Programming with F# is easy

Practical Guide to F#

V.Telman

Copyright © 2024

Guide to F#

1. Introduction to F#

F# (pronounced "F Sharp") is a functional-first programming language developed by Microsoft as part of the .NET family. It combines functional, imperative, and object-oriented programming paradigms, making it a versatile and powerful tool for software development. F# is designed to handle a wide range of programming tasks, from scripting and web development to scientific computing and financial modeling. Its strong type system, concise syntax, and powerful abstractions make it a popular choice among developers who value code clarity, maintainability, and expressiveness.

What is F# and Why Learn It?

Functional Programming Paradigm:

F# is primarily a functional programming language, which means it emphasizes the use of immutable data, first-class functions, and expressions rather than statements. This approach leads to more predictable and testable code, reducing the likelihood of bugs and making programs easier to reason about. Functional programming encourages developers to think in terms of transformations and compositions, which can lead to cleaner and more modular code.

Versatility:

While F# is functional-first, it seamlessly integrates with object-oriented and imperative programming paradigms. This allows developers to use the most appropriate paradigm for a given task. For instance, F# can leverage object-oriented features when dealing with .NET libraries and frameworks or switch to an imperative style for performance-critical sections of code.

Concise and Expressive Syntax:

F# is known for its concise and expressive syntax, which reduces boilerplate code and improves readability. Its powerful type inference system allows developers to write less code while still maintaining type safety. This results in more maintainable and easier-to-understand codebases.

Interoperability:

F# is part of the .NET ecosystem, which means it can interoperate with other .NET languages like C# and Visual Basic. This interoperability allows F# to leverage the vast array of .NET libraries and tools, making it suitable for a wide range of applications, from web development to data analysis.

Concurrency and Parallelism:

Functional programming languages like F# are well-suited for concurrent and parallel programming. Immutability and the absence of side effects make it easier to write safe and efficient concurrent code. F# provides robust support for asynchronous programming through features like asynchronous workflows and the `Async` type, which facilitate the development of responsive and scalable applications.

Strong Community and Support:

F# has a vibrant and growing community of developers who contribute to its ecosystem through libraries, tools, and educational resources. The language is actively maintained and supported by Microsoft, ensuring it evolves to meet the needs of modern software development.

Applications in Various Domains:

F# is used in diverse fields such as finance, gaming, data science, and web development. Its ability to handle complex data transformations, mathematical computations, and real-time processing makes it a popular choice for financial modeling, scientific research, and high-performance computing.

History of F#

F# was created by Don Syme at Microsoft Research in 2005 as a research project aimed at exploring functional programming on the .NET platform. The language was inspired by OCaml, a functional programming language from the ML family, and aimed to bring the benefits of functional programming to the .NET ecosystem.

Early Development and Release:

The development of F# began in the early 2000s, with Don Syme and his team at Microsoft Research working on the language. The goal was to create a language that could leverage the .NET runtime while promoting functional programming principles. F# drew heavily from OCaml, adopting its type system, pattern matching, and functional constructs.

In 2007, F# 1.0 was released as an official Microsoft language, marking its transition from a research project to a fully-supported programming language. This release included integration with Visual Studio, making it easier for developers to adopt F# for .NET applications.

Growth and Adoption:

F# continued to evolve, with subsequent releases introducing new features and improvements. The language gained traction in the .NET community and beyond, particularly among developers interested in functional programming. F# 2.0, released in 2010, introduced significant enhancements, including improved type inference, support for parallel and asynchronous programming, and better integration with .NET libraries.

The release of F# 3.0 in 2012 brought further advancements, such as Type Providers, which enable seamless access to external data sources, and query expressions, which simplify data manipulation. These features made F# even more attractive for data-centric applications and reinforced its position as a versatile and powerful language.

Open Source and Cross-Platform Development:

In 2014, Microsoft open-sourced F# and its

compiler, allowing the community to contribute to its development and ensuring greater transparency. This move also facilitated the language's adoption across different platforms, including Linux and macOS, through the Mono and .NET Core frameworks.

The release of .NET Core, a cross-platform, open-source version of the .NET framework, further boosted F#'s popularity by enabling developers to build and deploy F# applications on various operating systems. The combination of F#'s functional programming capabilities and the flexibility of .NET Core has made it a compelling choice for modern software development.

Recent Developments:

F# continues to evolve with regular updates and new features. Recent versions have focused on enhancing performance, improving interoperability with other .NET languages, and expanding the language's capabilities for modern development practices. The introduction of F# 5.0 in 2020 brought several new features, including improved pattern matching, enhanced interop with C#, and better support for high-performance computing.

The F# community remains active, with contributions from both Microsoft and independent developers driving the language forward. The availability of comprehensive documentation, tutorials, and community-driven projects ensures that F# remains accessible and relevant to new generations of developers.

Advantages of Using F#

1. Functional Programming Benefits:

F# promotes functional programming principles, which offer several advantages for software development. Functional programming emphasizes immutability, first-class functions, and pure functions (functions without side effects), leading to code that is easier to understand, test, and maintain.

- **Immutability:** In F#, data is typically immutable, meaning it cannot be changed once created. This reduces the likelihood of unintended side effects and makes it easier to reason about code behavior. Immutable data structures are inherently thread-safe, simplifying concurrent and parallel programming.

- **First-Class Functions:** Functions are first-class citizens in F#, meaning they can be passed as arguments, returned from other functions, and assigned to variables. This enables powerful abstractions and code reuse through higher-order functions and function composition.

- **Pure Functions:** Pure functions produce the same output for the same input and do not have side effects, making them predictable and easy to test. Pure functions facilitate functional programming's declarative style, where developers describe what to compute rather than how to compute it.

2. Strong Type System:

F# features a strong, statically-typed system that provides several benefits:

- **Type Safety:** The type system catches many errors at compile time, reducing runtime errors and increasing code reliability. Type safety ensures that operations are performed on compatible data types, preventing common bugs such as null reference exceptions.

- **Type Inference:** F# has an advanced type inference system that reduces the need for explicit type annotations. The compiler can often deduce the types of variables and expressions, resulting in more concise and readable code without sacrificing type safety.

- **Pattern Matching:** Pattern matching is a powerful feature in F# that allows developers to deconstruct data types and perform actions based on their structure. It simplifies complex data manipulations and enhances code readability by making intent explicit.

3. Interoperability with .NET:

As part of the .NET ecosystem, F# can seamlessly interoperate with other .NET languages like C# and Visual Basic. This interoperability provides access to a vast array of libraries and frameworks, enabling F# developers to leverage existing .NET resources.

- **Library Access:** F# can use any .NET library, allowing developers to take advantage of mature libraries for tasks such as web development (ASP.NET), data access (Entity Framework), and user interface design (WPF, WinForms).

- **Tooling:** F# benefits from the robust tooling available in the .NET ecosystem. Integrated development environments (IDEs) like Visual Studio and JetBrains Rider provide features such as IntelliSense, debugging, and project templates, enhancing developer productivity.

4. Asynchronous and Concurrent Programming:

F# excels in asynchronous and concurrent programming, making it suitable for developing responsive and scalable applications.

- **Asynchronous Workflows:** F# provides native support for asynchronous programming through asynchronous workflows (`async` keyword) and the `Async` type. This simplifies the development of non-blocking I/O operations, such as network requests and file operations, improving application responsiveness.

- **Concurrency:** Functional programming's emphasis on immutability and pure functions makes it easier to write concurrent code without the pitfalls of shared mutable state. F#'s support for message-passing concurrency models, such as the actor model (e.g., Akka.NET), further simplifies concurrent programming.

5. Domain-Specific Languages (DSLs):

F#'s expressive syntax and powerful type system make it well-suited for creating domain-specific languages (DSLs). DSLs allow developers to define custom languages tailored to specific problem domains, improving code readability and maintainability.

- **Custom Operators:** F# supports custom operators, enabling developers to create concise and readable syntax for DSLs. Custom operators can represent domain-specific concepts, making the code more intuitive for domain experts.

- **Active Patterns:** Active patterns allow developers to define custom pattern-matching rules, facilitating the creation of DSLs that can match and deconstruct complex data structures in a natural way.

6. Data Processing and Analysis:

F# is widely used in data processing and analysis due to its powerful abstractions and ability to handle complex data transformations.

- **Type Providers:** Type Providers are a unique feature of F# that enable the integration of external data sources directly into the type system. They provide compile-time access to structured data, such as databases, web services, and file formats, simplifying data access and manipulation.

- **Data Frames and Series:** F# has libraries like Deedle that provide data frame and series structures, similar to those in R and Python's pandas. These libraries facilitate data manipulation, exploration, and analysis, making F# a viable choice for data science and analytics.

7. Financial and Scientific Computing:

F# is well-regarded in the finance and scientific communities for its ability to handle complex mathematical computations and large datasets.

- **Numerical Computing:** F# supports libraries like Math.NET Numerics and F# for Numerics, which provide tools for numerical computing, linear algebra, and statistical analysis. These libraries enable the development of high-performance applications for scientific research and financial modeling.

- **Algorithmic Trading:** F#'s functional programming capabilities and strong type system make it suitable for developing algorithmic trading systems. The language's expressiveness allows traders to implement and test trading strategies efficiently, while its performance characteristics ensure timely execution of trades.

8. Web Development:

F# can be used for web development, offering several frameworks and tools that leverage its functional programming capabilities.

- **SAFE Stack:** The SAFE Stack is a full-stack web development framework for F# that combines Suave (web server), Azure, Fable (F# to JavaScript compiler), and Elmish (model-view-update architecture). The SAFE Stack enables the development of modern web applications with a functional programming approach, promoting code reuse and maintainability.

- **ASP.NET Core:** F# integrates with ASP.NET Core, Microsoft's cross-platform web framework. This allows developers to build web APIs, MVC applications, and real-time web applications using F# while benefiting from the performance and scalability of ASP.NET Core.

9. Community and Ecosystem:

F# has a vibrant and supportive community that contributes to its ecosystem through libraries, tools, and educational resources.

- **Open Source:** F# and its core libraries are open source, encouraging community contributions and collaboration. This open-source nature ensures that the language remains relevant and continues to evolve to meet the needs of developers.

- **Learning Resources:** The F# community provides a wealth of learning resources, including tutorials, documentation, online courses, and books. These resources help new developers get started with F# and enable experienced developers to deepen their knowledge.

- **Community Projects:** The F# community maintains a variety of open-source projects that extend the language's capabilities. Libraries like FsCheck (property-based testing), FParsec (parser combinators), and Giraffe (functional ASP.NET Core framework) demonstrate the language's versatility and foster innovation.

F# is a powerful and versatile programming language that offers the benefits of functional programming while seamlessly integrating with the .NET ecosystem. Its strong type system, concise syntax, and robust support for asynchronous and concurrent programming make it a compelling choice for modern software development. F# is used in diverse domains, from financial modeling and scientific computing to web development and data analysis. With a vibrant community and strong support from Microsoft, F# continues to evolve and provide developers with the tools they need to build reliable, maintainable, and scalable applications.

2. Guide to Installing F#

F# is a powerful functional-first programming language that runs on the .NET platform. Installing F# involves setting up the .NET SDK, which includes the F# compiler and the runtime environment necessary to execute F# applications. This guide provides step-by-step instructions to install F# on Windows, macOS, and Linux, along with setting up your development environment using popular IDEs and editors.

Installing F# on Windows

1. **Install .NET SDK:**

   - Visit the [.NET Download page] (https://dotnet.microsoft.com/download).

   - Download the .NET SDK installer for Windows.

   - Run the installer and follow the instructions to complete the installation.

2. **Verify Installation:**

   - Open a command prompt.

   - Type `dotnet --version` to verify that .NET SDK is installed correctly. You should see the version number of the installed SDK.

3. **Install Visual Studio (Optional):**

   - Download and install [Visual Studio] (https://visualstudio.microsoft.com/).

   - During the installation, select the ".NET desktop development" workload. This workload includes support for F#.

   - Open Visual Studio and create a new F# project to get started.

4. **Using Visual Studio Code:**

   - Download and install [Visual Studio Code] (https://code.visualstudio.com/).

   - Open Visual Studio Code.

- Install the Ionide extension for F# by searching for "Ionide" in the Extensions view (Ctrl+Shift+X) and clicking "Install."

Installing F# on macOS

1. **Install .NET SDK:**

   - Visit the [.NET Download page] (https://dotnet.microsoft.com/download).

   - Download the .NET SDK installer for macOS.

   - Open the `.pkg` file and follow the instructions to complete the installation.

2. **Verify Installation:**

   - Open the Terminal.

   - Type `dotnet --version` to verify that .NET SDK is installed correctly. You should see the version number of the installed SDK.

3. **Install Visual Studio for Mac (Optional):**

   - Download and install [Visual Studio for Mac](https://visualstudio.microsoft.com/vs/mac/).

   - Open Visual Studio for Mac and create a new F# project to get started.

4. **Using Visual Studio Code:**

   - Download and install [Visual Studio Code](https://code.visualstudio.com/).

   - Open Visual Studio Code.

   - Install the Ionide extension for F# by searching for "Ionide" in the Extensions view (Cmd+Shift+X) and clicking "Install."

Installing F# on Linux

1. **Install .NET SDK:**

   - Visit the [.NET Download page](https://dotnet.microsoft.com/download).

- Select your Linux distribution and follow the specific instructions provided.

For example, on Ubuntu:

```sh
wget https://packages.microsoft.com/config/ubuntu/20.04/packages-microsoft-prod.deb -O packages-microsoft-prod.deb

sudo dpkg -i packages-microsoft-prod.deb

sudo apt-get update; \

  sudo apt-get install -y apt-transport-https && \

  sudo apt-get update && \

  sudo apt-get install -y dotnet-sdk-5.0
```

2. **Verify Installation:**

   - Open a terminal.

   - Type `dotnet --version` to verify that .NET

SDK is installed correctly. You should see the version number of the installed SDK.

3. **Using Visual Studio Code:**

   - Download and install [Visual Studio Code](https://code.visualstudio.com/).

   - Open Visual Studio Code.

   - Install the Ionide extension for F# by searching for "Ionide" in the Extensions view (Ctrl+Shift+X) and clicking "Install."

Setting Up Your Development Environment

Regardless of your operating system, setting up a productive development environment is crucial for working with F#. Here are some recommendations:

1. **IDEs and Editors:**

   - **Visual Studio:** A comprehensive IDE

with excellent F# support, ideal for Windows and macOS users.

   - **Visual Studio Code:** A lightweight, cross-platform editor with robust support for F# via the Ionide extension.

   - **JetBrains Rider:** A powerful cross-platform IDE with excellent F# support, though it requires a subscription.

2. **Ionide Extension:**

   - Ionide is a popular extension for Visual Studio Code that provides comprehensive support for F# development, including syntax highlighting, IntelliSense, debugging, and project management.

   - Install Ionide from the Extensions view in Visual Studio Code by searching for "Ionide" and clicking "Install."

3. **Creating a New F# Project:**

   - Open your terminal or command prompt.

   - Use the following commands to create and

run a new F# project:

```sh

dotnet new console -lang F# -o MyFSharpApp

cd MyFSharpApp

dotnet run

```

4. **Running and Debugging F# Code:**

   - Visual Studio and Visual Studio Code (with Ionide) provide built-in debugging tools for F# projects.

   - Set breakpoints, inspect variables, and step through your code to debug effectively.

Additional Resources

- **Official Documentation:**

  - The [F# Documentation](https://docs.microsoft.com/en-us/dotnet/fsharp/) provides comprehensive guides, tutorials, and references for learning F#.

- **Community Resources:**

  - **F# Software Foundation (FSSF):** The [F# Software Foundation](https://fsharp.org/) offers community support, resources, and events for F# developers.

  - **F# Slack Community:** Join the [F# Slack Community](https://fsharp.org/guides/slack/) to connect with other F# developers, ask questions, and share knowledge.

- **Books and Tutorials:**

  - "Programming F# 4.0" by Chris Smith

  - "Functional Programming in F#" by Enrico Buonanno

  - Online courses and tutorials on platforms like Pluralsight, Udemy, and Coursera.

Installing F# is a straightforward process,

whether you're using Windows, macOS, or Linux. By setting up the .NET SDK and configuring a suitable development environment with Visual Studio, Visual Studio Code, or another preferred IDE, you can start leveraging the power of F# for your projects. With its functional-first approach, strong type system, and seamless integration with the .NET ecosystem, F# offers a productive and enjoyable programming experience.

3.Basic Syntax of F#: Variables and Data Types

F# is a strongly-typed, functional-first programming language that is part of the .NET family. It supports both functional and object-oriented programming paradigms, making it a versatile language for various types of applications. Understanding the basic syntax, especially how variables and data types work in F#, is essential for writing effective F# code. This comprehensive guide will cover the basics of variables and data types in F#, complete with examples to illustrate key concepts.

Variables in F#

In F#, variables are immutable by default, meaning once a value is assigned to a variable, it cannot be changed. This immutability helps ensure the predictability and reliability of your code. However, F# also supports mutable variables when necessary.

1. **Immutable Variables (let bindings):**

The `let` keyword is used to define immutable variables in F#. Here's a simple example:

```fsharp
let x = 10
let y = 20
let sum = x + y

printfn "The sum of x and y is %d" sum
```

In this example, `x`, `y`, and `sum` are immutable variables. The `printfn` function is used to print the sum to the console.

2. **Mutable Variables:**

To define mutable variables, you use the `let mutable` keyword. Mutable variables can be reassigned new values.

```fsharp
let mutable counter = 0

counter <- counter + 1
printfn "Counter: %d" counter

counter <- counter + 1
printfn "Counter: %d" counter
```

Here, `counter` is a mutable variable. The `<-` operator is used to update its value.

3. **Functions and Immutability:**

In F#, functions can also be defined using the `let` keyword, and they follow the same immutability principles.

```fsharp
let add a b = a + b

let result = add 5 3
printfn "The result is %d" result
```

In this example, `add` is a function that takes two arguments and returns their sum. The `result` variable is then used to store the result of calling the `add` function.

Data Types in F#

F# has a rich type system that includes both

primitive and complex data types. The type of a variable is usually inferred by the compiler, but it can also be explicitly specified.

1. **Primitive Data Types:**

   - **Integers:**

   F# supports several integer types, including `int`, `int8`, `int16`, `int32`, and `int64`. The `int` type is an alias for `int32`.

   ```fsharp
   let intValue: int = 42
   let int8Value: int8 = 127y
   let int16Value: int16 = 32767s
   let int64Value: int64 = 9223372036854775807L
   ```

- **Floating-Point Numbers:**

F# supports single-precision (`float32`) and double-precision (`float`) floating-point numbers.

```fsharp
let floatValue: float = 3.14
let float32Value: float32 = 2.718f
```

- **Booleans:**

The boolean type in F# is `bool`, with two possible values: `true` and `false`.

```fsharp
let isFSharpFun: bool = true
```

- **Characters:**

The `char` type represents a single character.

```fsharp
let letter: char = 'F'
```

- **Strings:**

Strings in F# are represented by the `string` type and can be defined using double quotes.

```fsharp
let greeting: string = "Hello, F#"
```

2. **Unit Type:**

The unit type `unit` is used to represent the absence of a value. It's similar to `void` in other languages.

```fsharp
let printMessage () =
    printfn "This is a message"
    ()

printMessage ()
```

The `printMessage` function returns `unit`, indicating it doesn't return any meaningful value.

3. **Tuples:**

Tuples are used to group multiple values together. They can hold values of different types.

```fsharp
let coordinates = (10, 20)
let person = ("John", 30, true)

let (x, y) = coordinates
printfn "X: %d, Y: %d" x y

let (name, age, isEmployed) = person
printfn "Name: %s, Age: %d, Employed: %b" name age isEmployed
```

In this example, `coordinates` is a tuple of two integers, and `person` is a tuple containing a string, an integer, and a boolean.

4. **Records:**

Records are used to define composite data types with named fields.

```fsharp
type Person = {
    Name: string
    Age: int
    IsEmployed: bool
}


let john = { Name = "John"; Age = 30; IsEmployed = true }

printfn "Name: %s, Age: %d, Employed: %b" john.Name john.Age john.IsEmployed
```

Here, `Person` is a record type with three fields: `Name`, `Age`, and `IsEmployed`. The `john` variable is an instance of the `Person` record.

5. **Discriminated Unions:**

Discriminated unions are used to define types that can represent multiple distinct cases.

```fsharp
type Shape =
    | Circle of float
    | Rectangle of float * float

let area shape =
    match shape with
    | Circle radius -> System.Math.PI * radius * radius
```

```
    | Rectangle (width, height) -> width * height

    let circle = Circle 5.0
    let rectangle = Rectangle (4.0, 6.0)

    printfn "Area of the circle: %f" (area circle)
    printfn "Area of the rectangle: %f" (area rectangle)
```

In this example, `Shape` is a discriminated union with two cases: `Circle` and `Rectangle`. The `area` function calculates the area based on the shape type.

6. **Option Type:**

The `option` type is used to represent values that may or may not exist. It's commonly used to handle nullability in a type-safe manner.

```fsharp
let divide x y =
    if y = 0 then None
    else Some (x / y)

let result = divide 10 2
match result with
| Some value -> printfn "Result: %d" value
| None -> printfn "Cannot divide by zero"
```

Here, `divide` returns an `option<int>` that is either `Some` with the result or `None` if division by zero occurs.

7. **Lists:**

Lists are immutable collections that are frequently used in F# for functional programming tasks.

```fsharp
let numbers = [1; 2; 3; 4; 5]

let sum = List.sum numbers
printfn "Sum of numbers: %d" sum

let doubledNumbers = List.map (fun x -> x * 2) numbers
printfn "Doubled numbers: %A" doubledNumbers
```

In this example, `numbers` is a list of integers. The `List.sum` function calculates the sum, and `List.map` is used to create a new list with each number doubled.

8. **Arrays:**

Arrays are mutable collections of elements of the same type.

```fsharp
let numbersArray = [| 1; 2; 3; 4; 5 |]

numbersArray.[0] <- 10
printfn "First element: %d" numbersArray.[0]


let squares = Array.map (fun x -> x * x) numbersArray
printfn "Squares: %A" squares
```

Here, `numbersArray` is an array of integers. The element at index 0 is modified, and `Array.map` is used to create a new array of squared numbers.

9. **Sequences:**

Sequences (`seq`) are lazy collections that are computed on demand.

```fsharp
let numbersSeq = seq { 1 .. 10 }

let evens = Seq.filter (fun x -> x % 2 = 0) numbersSeq

printfn "Even numbers: %A" evens
```

In this example, `numbersSeq` is a sequence of numbers from 1 to 10. The `Seq.filter` function creates a new sequence containing only even numbers.

10. **Maps:**

Maps are immutable collections of key-value pairs.

```fsharp
let capitals = Map.ofList [ ("USA", "Washington, D.C."); ("UK", "London"); ("France", "Paris") ]

match capitals.TryFind "USA" with
| Some capital -> printfn "Capital of USA: %s" capital
| None -> printfn "Not found"
```

Here, `capitals` is a map created from a list of key-value pairs. The `TryFind` method is used to safely retrieve the value associated with a key.

Pattern Matching

Pattern matching is a powerful feature in F# that allows you to decompose and analyze data structures.

1. **Basic Pattern Matching:**

```fsharp
let describeNumber x =
    match x with
    | 0 -> "Zero"
    | 1 -> "One"
    | _ -> "Other"

printfn "%s" (describeNumber 1)
```

```

In this example, the `describeNumber` function uses pattern matching to return a description of the input number.

2. **Pattern Matching with Tuples:**

```fsharp
let swap (a, b) = (b, a)

let original = (1, 2)
let swapped = swap original

printfn "Original: %A, Swapped: %A" original swapped
```

Here, the `swap` function swaps the
```

elements of a tuple using pattern matching.

3. **Pattern Matching with Lists:**

```fsharp
let rec sumList lst =
    match lst with
    | [] -> 0
    | head :: tail -> head + sumList tail

let numbers = [1; 2; 3; 4; 5]
let total = sumList numbers

printfn "Sum of list: %d" total
```

In this example, `sumList` is a recursive function that sums the elements of a list using pattern matching.

Understanding the basic syntax of F#, particularly how variables and data types work, is essential for leveraging the language's powerful functional programming capabilities. This guide covered immutable and mutable variables, primitive and complex data types, and demonstrated how to use them effectively with pattern matching and other F# features. By mastering these concepts, you'll be well-equipped to write efficient and expressive F# code.

4. Fuctions

In F#, functions are first-class citizens, which means they can be treated just like any other data type. Functions in F# can take multiple arguments, return a value, and be assigned to variables. They can also be passed as arguments to other functions and returned as values from other functions.

Here are some examples of functions in F#:

1. Simple function:
```fsharp
let add x y = x + y
```
This function takes two arguments, x and y, and returns their sum.

2. Higher-order function:
```fsharp
let applyFunc f x = f x
```
This function takes another function, f, as an argument and applies it to another argument, x. This allows you to pass any function to applyFunc and it will be applied to the input

x.

3. Recursive function:
```fsharp
let rec factorial n =
    if n = 0 then 1
    else n * factorial (n - 1)
```

This function calculates the factorial of a given number using recursion. It calls itself with a smaller input until it reaches the base case of n = 0.

4. Anonymous function:
```fsharp
let double = fun x -> x * 2
```

This defines an anonymous function that doubles the input value. Anonymous functions are useful for creating short, one-time use functions.

5. Partial application:
```fsharp
let add1 = add 1
```

This creates a new function, add1, by partially

applying the add function with the argument 1. This can be useful for creating specialized functions from more general ones.

6. Currying:
```fsharp
let addCurried x y = x + y
```

This function takes two arguments like the simple add function, but it is automatically curried. This means that you can pass one argument at a time to addCurried, creating a chain of functions.

7. Composition:
```fsharp
let square x = x * x
let doubleThenSquare = square >> double
```

This example shows function composition using the pipeline operator (>>). The doubleThenSquare function first doubles the input value and then squares the result.

8. Pattern matching:
```fsharp
let rec fibonacci n =
```

```
    match n with
    | 0 | 1 -> n
    | _ -> fibonacci (n - 1) + fibonacci (n - 2)
```

This function calculates the nth Fibonacci number using pattern matching. It handles different cases based on the value of n, making the code more readable and concise.

9. List manipulation:
```fsharp
let sumList list = List.sum list
let evens = List.filter (fun x -> x % 2 = 0)
```

These functions demonstrate how to manipulate lists in F#. The sumList function calculates the sum of all elements in a list, while the evens function filters out even numbers from a list.

10. Tail recursion optimization:
```fsharp
let rec factorialTail n acc =
    if n = 0 then acc
    else factorialTail (n - 1) (n * acc)
let factorial n = factorialTail n 1
```

This function calculates the factorial of a number using tail recursion, which is more efficient than regular recursion. It uses an accumulator parameter to accumulate the result as it recurses through the function.

These examples showcase the versatility and power of functions in F#. By leveraging features like higher-order functions, recursion, pattern matching, and function composition, you can create expressive and concise code for a wide range of problems. Functions play a central role in functional programming languages like F#, enabling you to write clean, modular, and maintainable code.

5. Pattern matching and List comprehension

Pattern matching is a powerful feature in F# that allows developers to deconstruct complex data structures and make decisions based on the shape or content of the data. It is commonly used in functions and expressions to match different cases and perform specific actions accordingly.

One common example of pattern matching in F# is matching on discriminated unions. Discriminated unions are a way to define a data type that can have different cases, each with its own set of data or parameters. For example, consider a simple discriminated union representing different shapes:

```fsharp
type Shape =
    | Circle of float
    | Rectangle of float * float
    | Square of float
```

With this definition, we can create instances of different shapes and use pattern matching to perform actions based on the specific shape. For instance, we can define a function that calculates the area of a shape:

```fsharp
let calculateArea shape =
    match shape with
    | Circle(radius) -> Math.PI * radius * radius
    | Rectangle(width, height) -> width * height
    | Square(side) -> side * side
```

In this function, we match on the different cases of the Shape type using the `match` keyword. For each case, we destructure the data and perform the appropriate calculation to calculate the area.

Another common use case for pattern matching is in handling lists. List comprehension is a feature in F# that allows developers to create new lists by applying transformations to existing lists. Combined with pattern matching, list comprehension becomes a powerful tool for filtering and transforming lists based on specific criteria.

For example, let's say we have a list of integers and we want to filter out even numbers and square the odd numbers:

```fsharp
let numbers = [1; 2; 3; 4; 5]

let transformedNumbers =
    [ for number in numbers do
        match number with
        | n when n % 2 = 0 -> None
        | n -> Some(n * n) ]
    |> List.choose id
```

In this example, we use list comprehension to iterate over each number in the original list. We then use pattern matching within the `match` expression to check if the number is even or odd. For even numbers, we return `None` which effectively filters them out. For odd numbers, we return `Some(n * n)` which squares them. Finally, we use `List.choose id` to filter out the `None` values and keep only the squared odd numbers in the `transformedNumbers` list.

Overall, pattern matching and list comprehension are powerful features in F# that allow developers to write concise and expressive code for handling complex data structures and performing transformations on lists. By leveraging these features, developers can write clean and efficient code that is easy to understand and maintain.

6. Record and tuple

In F#, records and tuples are two fundamental data types that are commonly used for storing and manipulating structured data. Each has its own distinct characteristics and use cases, making them important tools for working with data in F#.

Records in F# are similar to classes in object-oriented programming languages, but with some key differences. Records are immutable data structures that are defined using the ```type``` keyword, followed by the name of the record and a list of fields enclosed in curly braces. Each field in a record is defined with a label and a type, separated by a colon. Here's an example of a simple record definition in F#:

```
type Person = {
   FirstName: string;
   LastName: string;
   Age: int;
}
```

```

In this example, we have defined a record type called ```Person``` with three fields: ```FirstName```, ```LastName```, and ```Age```. Each field has a specific type, such as ```string``` for the name fields and ```int``` for the age field. Records in F# provide a convenient way to group related data fields together and are often used to represent entities in a domain model.

Records in F# are immutable by default, meaning that once a record is created, its fields cannot be modified. Instead, F# encourages a functional programming style where new records are created by copying existing records and updating specific fields as needed. This helps prevent unintended side effects and makes it easier to reason about code.

To create an instance of a record in F#, you can use the following syntax:

```

let person1 = { FirstName = "John";

LastName = "Doe"; Age = 30 }
```

This creates a new instance of the ```Person``` record with the specified values for each field. Once a record has been created, you can access its fields using the dot notation:

```
printfn "Name: %s %s, Age: %d" person1.FirstName person1.LastName person1.Age
```

Records in F# can also have properties and methods defined on them, just like classes in object-oriented languages. This allows you to encapsulate behavior along with data and create reusable components.

Tuples, on the other hand, are lightweight data structures in F# that can hold a fixed number of elements of different types. Tuples are created using parentheses and commas to separate the elements, with the type of the tuple inferred based on its elements. Here's an example of a tuple in F#:
```

```
let personTuple = ("John", "Doe", 30)
```

In this example, we have created a tuple with three elements representing the first name, last name, and age of a person. Tuples in F# are commonly used for temporary data storage or as a way to return multiple values from a function.

Unlike records, tuples in F# are mutable and are typically used in situations where a simple data structure is needed for holding a fixed number of values. Tuples are often used in F# to represent pairs or triples of values in a concise and flexible manner.

To access the elements of a tuple in F#, you can use pattern matching or deconstruction syntax:

```
let (firstName, lastName, age) = personTuple

printfn "Name: %s %s, Age: %d" firstName
```

lastName age
```

This syntax allows you to extract the individual elements of the tuple and bind them to variables for further processing. Tuples in F# are a convenient way to work with multiple values as a single unit, without the need to define a custom data type like records.

In summary, records and tuples are two important data types in F# that provide different ways of structuring and manipulating data. Records are immutable data structures that are used to represent complex entities with named fields, while tuples are lightweight structures for holding a fixed number of values of different types. By understanding the strengths and limitations of records and tuples, you can effectively model and manipulate data in F# programs.
```

7.If-then-else e match

In F#, like in many programming languages, we have structures like if-then-else and match to control the flow of our code. These structures allow us to make decisions based on certain conditions, allowing our programs to be more flexible and dynamic.

Let's start by exploring the if-then-else structure in F#. This structure is used to execute certain code blocks based on whether a certain condition is true or false. The syntax for if-then-else in F# is as follows:

```fsharp
if condition then
    // code to execute if condition is true
else
    // code to execute if condition is false
```

For example, let's say we want to check if a number is even or odd:

```fsharp
```

```
let num = 10
if num % 2 = 0 then
    printfn "The number is even"
else
    printfn "The number is odd"
```

In this example, if the condition `num % 2 = 0` is true, the program will print "The number is even", otherwise it will print "The number is odd".

Next, let's move on to the match structure in F#. This structure is used to match a value against a series of patterns and execute the corresponding code block based on the matched pattern. The syntax for match in F# is as follows:

```fsharp
match value with
| pattern1 -> // code to execute if value matches pattern1
| pattern2 -> // code to execute if value matches pattern2
| _ -> // code to execute if value doesn't match any pattern
```

```

For example, let's say we want to match a number against different ranges:

```fsharp
let num = 5
match num with
| n when n < 0 -> printfn "The number is negative"
| n when n > 0 && n <= 10 -> printfn "The number is between 1 and 10"
| _ -> printfn "The number is greater than 10"
```

In this example, the value of `num` is matched against different patterns to determine in which range the number falls. Depending on the matched pattern, the corresponding message will be printed.

Both if-then-else and match structures are powerful tools that allow us to write more expressive and concise code in F#. By using these structures effectively, we can make our programs more readable and maintainable,
```

while also adding dynamic behavior based on certain conditions.

8. Recursion

The concept of recursion in programming is essential for solving problems that can be defined in terms of simpler versions of themselves. In functional programming languages like F#, recursion is a powerful tool for writing concise and elegant code. In this guide, we will explore the concept of recursion in F# with simple examples to help you understand how it works.

Recursion is a technique where a function calls itself in order to solve a problem. This process continues until a base case is reached, at which point the function stops calling itself and begins returning values back up the call stack.

Let's start with a simple example of a recursive function in F#, the factorial function. The factorial of a non-negative integer n is the product of all positive integers less than or equal to n. We can define the factorial function recursively as follows:

```fsharp
let rec factorial n =
   if n = 0 then 1
   else n * factorial (n - 1)
```

In this function, we first check if n is equal to 0. If it is, we return 1 because the factorial of 0 is 1. Otherwise, we multiply n by the factorial of (n-1) to compute the factorial of n.

To better understand how recursion works, let's walk through an example using the factorial function. Suppose we want to compute the factorial of 5:

```
factorial 5
5 * factorial 4
5 * (4 * factorial 3)
5 * (4 * (3 * factorial 2))
5 * (4 * (3 * (2 * factorial 1)))
5 * (4 * (3 * (2 * (1 * factorial 0))))
5 * (4 * (3 * (2 * (1 * 1))))
5 * (4 * (3 * (2 * 1)))
5 * (4 * (3 * 2))
5 * (4 * 6)
```

```
5 * 24
120
```

As you can see, the function calls itself multiple times until it reaches the base case (n = 0), at which point it starts returning values back up the call stack to compute the final result.

Recursion can also be used to solve more complex problems. For example, let's consider the Fibonacci sequence, where each number is the sum of the two preceding ones (starting from 0 and 1). We can define a recursive function to compute the nth Fibonacci number as follows:

```fsharp
let rec fibonacci n =
    match n with
    | 0 -> 0
    | 1 -> 1
    | _ -> fibonacci (n-1) + fibonacci (n-2)
```

In this function, we use pattern matching to

handle the base cases where n is equal to 0 or 1. For any other value of n, we recursively calculate the (n-1)th Fibonacci number and the (n-2)th Fibonacci number, and then add them together to get the nth Fibonacci number.

Let's walk through an example using the Fibonacci function to compute the 6th Fibonacci number:

```
fibonacci 6
fibonacci 5 + fibonacci 4
(fibonacci 4 + fibonacci 3) + (fibonacci 3 + fibonacci 2)
((fibonacci 3 + fibonacci 2) + (fibonacci 2 + fibonacci 1)) + ((fibonacci 2 + fibonacci 1) + fibonacci 0)
(((fibonacci 2 + fibonacci 1) + fibonacci 0) + (fibonacci 1 + 1)) + ((fibonacci 1 + 1) + 0)
(((1 + 1) + 0) + 1) + (1 + 0)
(2 + 1) + 1
3 + 1
4
```

Recursion is a powerful technique for solving

problems in functional programming languages like F#. However, it is important to ensure that recursive functions have well-defined base cases to avoid infinite loops. Additionally, recursive functions can sometimes be less efficient than iterative solutions, so it is important to consider the trade-offs when using recursion.

In conclusion, recursion is a fundamental concept in functional programming languages like F#, and it can be used to solve a wide range of problems in a concise and elegant manner. By understanding how recursion works and practicing writing recursive functions, you can become a more proficient F# programmer and leverage the power of recursion in your code.

9. higher-order functions

In F#, higher-order functions are functions that can take other functions as arguments or return a function as a result. This allows for more flexible and powerful programming techniques, as functions can be treated as first-class citizens and manipulated like any other data type.

One common example of a higher-order function in F# is the "map" function. The map function takes a function and a list as arguments, applies the function to each element of the list, and returns a new list with the results. For example:

```fsharp
let square x = x * x
let numbers = [1; 2; 3; 4; 5]
let squaredNumbers = List.map square numbers // [1; 4; 9; 16; 25]
```

In this example, the "square" function is passed to the map function, which applies the function to each element of the "numbers" list and returns a new list with the squared values.

Another common higher-order function in F# is the "filter" function. The filter function takes a predicate function and a list as arguments, applies the predicate to each element of the list, and returns a new list containing only the elements that satisfy the predicate. For example:

```fsharp
let isEven x = x % 2 = 0
let numbers = [1; 2; 3; 4; 5]
let evenNumbers = List.filter isEven numbers // [2; 4]
```

In this example, the "isEven" function is passed to the filter function, which applies the function to each element of the "numbers" list and returns a new list containing only the even numbers.

Higher-order functions can also be used to create new functions on the fly using techniques like currying and partial application. Currying is the process of breaking down a function with multiple arguments into a series of functions that each take a single argument. For example:

```fsharp
let add x y = x + y
let addOne = add 1
let result = addOne 2 // 3
```

In this example, the "add" function takes two arguments, but by using partial application, we can create a new function, "addOne", that only takes one argument and has the value of the first argument preset to 1.

Higher-order functions in F# can also be used to compose functions together to create more complex functions. The "compose" function can be used to combine two functions into a new function that applies the functions in sequence. For example:

```fsharp
let addTwo x = x + 2
let square x = x * x
let addTwoAndSquare = (addTwo >> square)
```

```
let result = addTwoAndSquare 3 // 25
```

In this example, the "addTwoAndSquare" function is created by composing the "addTwo" and "square" functions. The resulting function first adds 2 to the input and then squares the result.

Higher-order functions are an important part of functional programming in F# as they allow for greater flexibility, code reuse, and modularity in code. By treating functions as first-class citizens, developers can take advantage of powerful programming techniques to create more expressive and concise code.

10. Asynchronous and Parallel Programming in F#

F# is a versatile language that offers robust support for both asynchronous and parallel programming. These capabilities are essential for writing efficient, responsive, and scalable applications. Asynchronous programming allows your application to perform non-blocking operations, improving responsiveness, while parallel programming enables the concurrent execution of tasks to leverage multi-core processors.

This comprehensive guide will cover the concepts, syntax, and examples of asynchronous and parallel programming in F#. By the end of this guide, you will have a deep understanding of how to effectively use these features to build high-performance applications.

Introduction to Asynchronous Programming

Asynchronous programming in F# is primarily handled using the `async` keyword and the `Async` module. Asynchronous workflows in F# are designed to be simple, composable, and efficient.

1. **Basic Asynchronous Workflow:**

An asynchronous workflow in F# is defined using the `async` keyword followed by a computation expression. Here's a simple example:

```fsharp
open System.Threading.Tasks

let fetchDataAsync (url: string) =
    async {
        printfn "Fetching data from %s..." url
        // Simulate a delay
```

```
        do! Async.Sleep 2000
        printfn "Data fetched from %s" url
        return "Data"
    }

let result = fetchDataAsync "http://example.com" |> Async.RunSynchronously
printfn "Result: %s" result
```

In this example, `fetchDataAsync` is an asynchronous function that simulates fetching data from a URL. The `Async.Sleep` function is used to introduce a delay, representing an asynchronous operation. The `do!` keyword is used to await the completion of the asynchronous operation. The `Async.RunSynchronously` function runs the asynchronous workflow synchronously for demonstration purposes.

2. **Composing Asynchronous Workflows:**

Asynchronous workflows can be composed using the `let!` and `do!` keywords, allowing you to chain multiple asynchronous operations together.

```fsharp
let fetchMultipleDataAsync (urls: string list) =
    async {
        for url in urls do
            let! data = fetchDataAsync url
            printfn "Data received: %s" data
    }


let urls = ["http://example1.com"; "http://example2.com"; "http://example3.com"]

fetchMultipleDataAsync urls |>
```

Async.RunSynchronously

```

In this example, `fetchMultipleDataAsync` fetches data from multiple URLs sequentially. The `let!` keyword is used to await the result of each `fetchDataAsync` call.

3. **Handling Exceptions in Asynchronous Workflows:**

Exceptions in asynchronous workflows can be handled using the `try...with` expression.

```fsharp
let fetchDataWithErrorHandlingAsync (url: string) =
    async {
        try
            printfn "Fetching data from %s..."

```fsharp
            url
                do! Async.Sleep 2000
                if url = "http://example2.com" then
                    failwith "Network error"
                printfn "Data fetched from %s" url
                return "Data"
            with
            | ex -> printfn "Error fetching data from %s: %s" url ex.Message
                    return "Error"
        }


fetchDataWithErrorHandlingAsync "http://example1.com" |>
Async.RunSynchronously |> printfn "Result: %s"

fetchDataWithErrorHandlingAsync "http://example2.com" |>
Async.RunSynchronously |> printfn "Result: %s"
```

```

In this example, `fetchDataWithErrorHandlingAsync` simulates a network error for a specific URL and handles the exception using the `try...with` expression.

#### Parallel Programming

Parallel programming in F# is achieved through the `Parallel` module, which provides functions for executing tasks concurrently on multiple threads.

1. **Basic Parallel Execution:**

The `Parallel.Invoke` function allows you to execute multiple actions in parallel.

```fsharp

```
open System.Threading.Tasks

let task1 () =
    printfn "Task 1 starting..."
    Task.Delay(2000).Wait()
    printfn "Task 1 completed."

let task2 () =
    printfn "Task 2 starting..."
    Task.Delay(3000).Wait()
    printfn "Task 2 completed."

Parallel.Invoke(task1, task2)
```
```

In this example, `task1` and `task2` are executed in parallel using `Parallel.Invoke`.
```

2. **Parallel for Loops:**

The `Parallel.For` function allows you to execute a parallel for loop.

```fsharp
let numbers = [| 1 .. 10 |]

Parallel.For(0, numbers.Length, fun i ->
    printfn "Processing number %d on thread %d" numbers.[i] (Thread.CurrentThread.ManagedThreadId)
    Thread.Sleep(1000)
) |> ignore
```

In this example, a parallel for loop processes an array of numbers, printing each number along with the thread ID.

3. **Parallel LINQ (PLINQ):**

Parallel LINQ (PLINQ) is an extension of LINQ that provides parallel query capabilities.

```fsharp
open System.Linq

let numbers = [| 1 .. 1000000 |]

let parallelQuery = numbers.AsParallel().Where(fun n -> n % 2 = 0).ToArray()

printfn "Number of even numbers: %d" parallelQuery.Length
```

In this example, a parallel query is used to filter even numbers from a large array.

4. **Parallel Aggregation:**

The `Parallel.ForEach` function can be used for parallel aggregation tasks.

```fsharp
let sumArray (arr: int[]) =
    let sum = ref 0
    Parallel.ForEach(arr, fun n ->
        Interlocked.Add(sum, n) |> ignore
    ) |> ignore
    !sum

let numbers = [| 1 .. 1000 |]
let sum = sumArray numbers

printfn "Sum of numbers: %d" sum
```

In this example, `Parallel.ForEach` is used to sum an array of numbers in parallel.

Combining Asynchronous and Parallel Programming

F# allows you to combine asynchronous and parallel programming to create highly efficient and responsive applications.

1. **Parallel Asynchronous Workflows:**

You can run multiple asynchronous workflows in parallel using the `Async.Parallel` function.

```fsharp
let fetchAllDataAsync (urls: string list) =
    urls
    |> List.map fetchDataAsync
```

```
    |> Async.Parallel
    |> Async.RunSynchronously


let urls = ["http://example1.com";
"http://example2.com";
"http://example3.com"]

let results = fetchAllDataAsync urls

results |> Array.iter (printfn "Result: %s")
```

In this example, `fetchAllDataAsync` fetches data from multiple URLs in parallel, improving the overall performance.

2. **Asynchronous Parallel For Loop:**

You can combine asynchronous workflows with a parallel for loop using `Async.Parallel` and `Async.StartAsTask`.

```fsharp
let processNumbersAsync (numbers: int[]) =
    numbers
    |> Array.map (fun n -> async {
        printfn "Processing number %d on thread %d" n (Thread.CurrentThread.ManagedThreadId)
        do! Async.Sleep 1000
    })
    |> Async.Parallel
    |> Async.RunSynchronously

let numbers = [| 1 .. 10 |]
processNumbersAsync numbers |> ignore
```

In this example, each number in the array is processed asynchronously in parallel, demonstrating the combination of asynchronous and parallel programming.

3. **Using Tasks for Parallel Asynchronous Operations:**

The `Task` class from the .NET framework can be used for parallel asynchronous operations.

```fsharp
open System.Threading.Tasks

let fetchDataWithTask (url: string) =
    Task.Run(fun () ->
        printfn "Fetching data from %s on thread %d" url (Thread.CurrentThread.ManagedThreadId)
        Task.Delay(2000).Wait()
        printfn "Data fetched from %s" url
        "Data"
    )
```

```fsharp
let urls = ["http://example1.com"; "http://example2.com"; "http://example3.com"]

let tasks = urls |> List.map fetchDataWithTask

let results = Task.WhenAll(tasks) |> Async.AwaitTask |> Async.RunSynchronously


results |> Array.iter (printfn "Result: %s")
```

In this example, `fetchDataWithTask` creates a `Task` for each URL, and `Task.WhenAll` waits for all tasks to complete.

Advanced Asynchronous and Parallel Patterns

F# supports advanced patterns for asynchronous and parallel programming, enabling you to build sophisticated and high-performance applications.

1. **Agent-Based Concurrency:**

Agents, also known as mailboxes, provide a message-passing concurrency model that helps manage state in concurrent applications.

```fsharp
type Agent<'T> = MailboxProcessor<'T>

let agent = Agent.Start(fun inbox ->
    let rec loop state =
        async {
            let! msg = inbox.Receive()
            printfn "Received: %s" msg
            return! loop (state + 1)
```

```
        }
    loop 0
)


agent.Post("Hello, Agent!")
agent.Post("How are you?")
```

In this example, an agent is created to handle messages asynchronously.

The `loop` function processes incoming messages and maintains state.

2. **Task-Based Parallel Library (TPL):**

The TPL provides a rich set of APIs for parallel programming, including data parallelism, task parallelism, and concurrent data structures.

```fsharp
let processDataInParallel (data: int[]) =
    data
    |> Array.Parallel.map (fun x -> x * x)
    |> Array.sum

let numbers = [| 1 .. 1000 |]
let result = processDataInParallel numbers

printfn "Sum of squares: %d" result
```

In this example, the `Array.Parallel.map` function is used to process data in parallel.

3. **Parallel Data Structures:**

F# supports parallel data structures such as `ConcurrentQueue`, `ConcurrentStack`, and `ConcurrentDictionary`.

```fsharp
open System.Collections.Concurrent

let concurrentQueue = ConcurrentQueue<int>()

Parallel.For(0, 10, fun i ->
    concurrentQueue.Enqueue(i)
) |> ignore

while not concurrentQueue.IsEmpty do
    match concurrentQueue.TryDequeue() with
    | true, value -> printfn "Dequeued: %d" value
    | false, _ -> ()
```

```

In this example, `ConcurrentQueue` is used to safely enqueue and dequeue elements in a parallel loop.

Asynchronous and parallel programming in F# allows you to build responsive, efficient, and scalable applications. By understanding and utilizing the asynchronous workflows, parallel execution, and advanced concurrency patterns provided by F#, you can leverage the full power of modern hardware and improve the performance of your applications.

This guide has covered the basics of asynchronous and parallel programming, including practical examples and advanced patterns. By mastering these concepts, you will be well-equipped to tackle complex concurrent programming challenges in F#.
```

11. Using Libraries and Frameworks in F#

F# is a powerful and versatile programming language that seamlessly integrates with the .NET ecosystem. This allows F# developers to leverage a vast array of libraries and frameworks for various application domains. In this detailed guide, we will explore the utilization of external libraries, integration with the .NET Framework, and working with SQL Server and other databases using F#.

Utilizzo di Librerie Esterne

Using external libraries is a common practice in software development to avoid reinventing the wheel and to leverage well-tested solutions. In F#, you can use a wide range of libraries available in the .NET ecosystem.

1. **Adding Dependencies with Paket and NuGet:**

F# projects commonly use Paket, a dependency manager, and NuGet, the official package manager for .NET, to manage external libraries.

Using Paket:

```sh
dotnet tool install paket --tool-path .paket
.paket/paket.exe init
.paket/paket.exe add nuget Newtonsoft.Json
```

This installs Paket, initializes it, and adds the `Newtonsoft.Json` library.

Using NuGet:

```sh
```

```
dotnet add package Newtonsoft.Json
```

This command adds the `Newtonsoft.Json` package to your F# project using NuGet.

2. **Consuming Libraries in F#:**

Once a library is added, you can use it in your F# code. For example, using `Newtonsoft.Json` to parse JSON:

```fsharp
open Newtonsoft.Json

type Person = { Name: string; Age: int }

let json = """{ "Name": "John", "Age": 30 }"""
```

```fsharp
let person =
JsonConvert.DeserializeObject<Person>(json)

printfn "Name: %s, Age: %d" person.Name person.Age
```

This code deserializes a JSON string into a `Person` object using `Newtonsoft.Json`.

3. **Using F#-specific Libraries:**

There are libraries specifically designed for F#. For example, FSharp.Data provides a variety of data access functionalities.

```fsharp
open FSharp.Data

let csv = CsvProvider<"""Name,Age
```

```
John,30
Jane,25""">.GetSample()

for row in csv.Rows do
    printfn "Name: %s, Age: %d" row.Name row.Age
```

This example uses FSharp.Data's CSV type provider to parse and work with CSV data.

Integrazione con .NET Framework

F# fully integrates with the .NET Framework, allowing you to use .NET libraries and frameworks seamlessly.

1. **Working with .NET Libraries:**

You can use .NET libraries such as System.Collections, System.IO, and others directly in F#.

```fsharp
open System.Collections.Generic

let list = List<string>()
list.Add("Hello")
list.Add("World")

for item in list do
    printfn "%s" item
```

This example demonstrates using the `List<T>` class from the `System.Collections.Generic` namespace.

2. **Creating and Using .NET Classes:**

You can create and use .NET-style classes and interfaces in F#.

```fsharp
type Person(name: string, age: int) =
    member this.Name = name
    member this.Age = age
    member this.Introduce() = printfn "Hi, I'm %s and I'm %d years old." name age

let john = Person("John", 30)
john.Introduce()
```

This example defines a `Person` class with properties and methods, demonstrating object-oriented programming in F#.

3. **Using LINQ in F#:**

LINQ (Language Integrated Query) can be used in F# for querying collections.

```fsharp
open System.Linq

let numbers = [| 1; 2; 3; 4; 5 |]
let evenNumbers = numbers.Where(fun n -> n % 2 = 0).ToArray()

printfn "Even numbers: %A" evenNumbers
```

This code demonstrates using LINQ to filter an array of numbers.

4. **Working with WPF for GUI Development:**

F# can be used with Windows Presentation Foundation (WPF) for building GUI applications.

```fsharp
open System
open System.Windows
open System.Windows.Controls

let window = Window(Title = "F# WPF", Width = 400.0, Height = 300.0)
let button = Button(Content = "Click Me")

button.Click.Add(fun _ -> MessageBox.Show("Hello, World!") |> ignore)
window.Content <- button
```

```
[<EntryPoint>]
let main argv =
    Application().Run(window) |> ignore
    0
```

This example creates a simple WPF application with a button that displays a message when clicked.

Utilizzo di F# con SQL Server e Database

Working with databases is a crucial aspect of many applications. F# provides several ways to interact with SQL Server and other databases.

1. **Using ADO.NET:**

ADO.NET is a set of classes in the .NET Framework that provides access to data sources.

```fsharp
open System.Data.SqlClient

let connectionString = "your-connection-string-here"
let query = "SELECT Name, Age FROM Persons"

use connection = new SqlConnection(connectionString)
connection.Open()

use command = new SqlCommand(query, connection)
use reader = command.ExecuteReader()
```

```
    while reader.Read() do
      printfn "Name: %s, Age: %d" (reader.GetString(0)) (reader.GetInt32(1))
```

This code connects to a SQL Server database, executes a query, and prints the results.

2. **Using FSharp.Data.SqlClient:**

FSharp.Data.SqlClient is a type provider for SQL Server that allows you to write type-safe queries.

```fsharp
open FSharp.Data

type GetPersons =
```

```
SqlCommandProvider<"SELECT Name, Age FROM Persons", connectionString>

let persons = GetPersons().Execute()

for person in persons do
    printfn "Name: %s, Age: %d" person.Name person.Age
```

This example uses the `SqlCommandProvider` to execute a SQL query and iterate over the results.

3. **Using Entity Framework Core:**

Entity Framework Core (EF Core) is a modern object-database mapper for .NET. It allows you to work with databases using .NET objects.

```fsharp
open Microsoft.EntityFrameworkCore

type Person = { Id: int; Name: string; Age: int }

type AppDbContext() =
    inherit DbContext()
    [<DefaultValue>]
    val mutable persons: DbSet<Person>
    member this.Persons with get() = this.persons and set v = this.persons <- v

    override this.OnConfiguring(optionsBuilder: DbContextOptionsBuilder) =
        optionsBuilder.UseSqlServer("your-connection-string-here") |> ignore

let addPerson (context: AppDbContext)
```

```fsharp
    (person: Person) =
        context.Persons.Add(person) |> ignore
        context.SaveChanges() |> ignore

    let fetchPersons (context: AppDbContext) =
        context.Persons.ToList()

    let person = { Id = 1; Name = "John"; Age = 30 }
    use context = new AppDbContext()
    addPerson context person

    let persons = fetchPersons context
    persons |> List.iter (fun p -> printfn "Name: %s, Age: %d" p.Name p.Age)
```

This code demonstrates using EF Core to add and fetch persons from a SQL Server database.

4. **Using Dapper:**

Dapper is a simple object mapper for .NET that helps you work with databases in a type-safe manner without the overhead of an ORM.

```fsharp
open System.Data.SqlClient

open Dapper


type Person = { Id: int; Name: string; Age: int }


let connectionString = "your-connection-string-here"


let fetchPersons () =
```

```
use connection = new SqlConnection(connectionString)

connection.Query<Person>("SELECT Id, Name, Age FROM Persons").AsList()


let persons = fetchPersons()

persons |> List.iter (fun p -> printfn "Name: %s, Age: %d" p.Name p.Age)
```

This example uses Dapper to query a SQL Server database and map the results to a list of `Person` objects.

Utilizing libraries and frameworks in F# enables you to leverage the rich ecosystem of .NET and build powerful applications efficiently. This guide covered the basics of adding and using external libraries, integrating with the .NET Framework, and working with SQL Server and databases using F#. By mastering these techniques, you can enhance your F# applications with robust functionality and ensure they meet the demands of modern software development.

Whether you're developing web applications, data-driven services, or desktop applications, the ability to integrate and utilize various libraries and frameworks is essential for building scalable and maintainable software solutions.

12. Designing Applications in F#

Designing applications in F# involves several key practices that help ensure the code is well-organized, maintainable, and efficient. This comprehensive guide will cover organizing your code, implementing unit tests, and performing debugging and profiling. By the end of this guide, you will have a thorough understanding of how to design robust applications in F#.

Organizzazione del Codice

Organizing your code effectively is essential for maintaining readability and scalability. F# provides several constructs to help you structure your code.

1. **Modules and Namespaces:**

Modules and namespaces are used to group

related functions, types, and values.

Modules:

```fsharp
module MathOperations =

    let add x y = x + y
    let subtract x y = x - y

printfn "Addition: %d" (MathOperations.add 5 3)
printfn "Subtraction: %d" (MathOperations.subtract 5 3)
```

Namespaces:

```fsharp
```

```fsharp
namespace MyApp.Utilities

module StringUtilities =

    let capitalize (str: string) =
        if String.IsNullOrEmpty(str) then str
        else str.Substring(0, 1).ToUpper() + str.Substring(1).ToLower()

printfn "Capitalized: %s" (MyApp.Utilities.StringUtilities.capitalize "hello")
```

2. **Organizing by Feature:**

Group related functionality together in modules or namespaces. For example, if you have a feature related to user management, you can create a module for it.

```fsharp
module UserManagement =

    type User = { Id: int; Name: string; Email: string }

    let createUser id name email =
        { Id = id; Name = name; Email = email }

    let getUserEmail user =
        user.Email

let user = UserManagement.createUser 1 "John Doe" "john.doe@example.com"
printfn "User Email: %s" (UserManagement.getUserEmail user)
```

3. **Separating Concerns:**

Use separate files and modules for different concerns (e.g., data access, business logic, presentation).

DataAccess.fs:

```fsharp
module DataAccess

let fetchData id =
    // Simulate fetching data from a database
    { Id = id; Name = "John Doe"; Email = "john.doe@example.com" }
```

BusinessLogic.fs:

```fsharp
module BusinessLogic

open DataAccess

let getUserDetails id =
    let user = fetchData id
    sprintf "Name: %s, Email: %s" user.Name user.Email
```

Main.fs:

```fsharp
open BusinessLogic

[<EntryPoint>]
```

```fsharp
let main argv =
    let userDetails = getUserDetails 1
    printfn "%s" userDetails
    0
```

4. **Using Type Providers:**

Type providers can simplify accessing external data sources and ensure type safety.

```fsharp
open FSharp.Data

type Users = JsonProvider<"""
[
    { "id": 1, "name": "John Doe", "email": "john.doe@example.com" },
    { "id": 2, "name": "Jane Doe", "email":
```

"jane.doe@example.com" }

]
""">

let users = Users.GetSample()

for user in users do
    printfn "User: %s, Email: %s" user.Name user.Email
```

5. **Functional Composition:**

Functional composition is a powerful feature in F# that allows you to build complex functions from simpler ones.

```fsharp
let add x y = x + y

```
let multiply x y = x * y

let addThenMultiply x y z =
  x |> add y |> multiply z

printfn "Result: %d" (addThenMultiply 2 3 4)  // (2 + 3) * 4 = 20
```

By organizing your code using these principles, you can create modular, maintainable, and readable applications.

Test Unitari

Unit testing is a crucial part of the development process that helps ensure your code is correct and reliable. F# has several testing frameworks available, including NUnit, xUnit, and Expecto.

1. **Setting Up a Testing Project:**

Create a new project for your tests and add the necessary dependencies. For example, using xUnit:

```sh
dotnet new xunit -n MyApp.Tests
dotnet add MyApp.Tests package xunit
dotnet add MyApp.Tests package FSharp.Core
```

2. **Writing Unit Tests:**

Create test modules and write your tests. Here's an example using xUnit:

```fsharp
namespace MyApp.Tests

open Xunit

module MathOperationsTests =

    [<Fact>]
    let ``Addition test`` () =
        let result = MathOperations.add 2 3
        Assert.Equal(5, result)

    [<Fact>]
    let ``Subtraction test`` () =
        let result = MathOperations.subtract 5 3
        Assert.Equal(2, result)
```

3. **Running Tests:**

   Run your tests using the .NET CLI:

   ```sh
   dotnet test MyApp.Tests
   ```

   This command will build and run your tests, providing a report of the results.

4. **Using Expecto for Testing:**

   Expecto is a testing framework designed specifically for F#. It provides a functional approach to testing.

   Adding Expecto:

```sh
dotnet add MyApp.Tests package Expecto
```

Writing Tests with Expecto:

```fsharp
open Expecto

[<Tests>]
let tests =
    testList "MathOperations Tests" [
        testCase "Addition test" <| fun _ ->
            let result = MathOperations.add 2 3
            Expect.equal result 5 "Should be equal to 5"

        testCase "Subtraction test" <| fun _ ->
```

```
            let result = MathOperations.subtract 5 3
            Expect.equal result 2 "Should be equal to 2"
    ]

[<EntryPoint>]
let main args =
    runTestsWithArgs defaultConfig args tests
```

5. **Using FsCheck for Property-Based Testing:**

FsCheck is a library for property-based testing in .NET, which helps you test the properties of your functions.

Adding FsCheck:

```sh
dotnet add MyApp.Tests package FsCheck
```

Writing Property-Based Tests:

```fsharp
open FsCheck
open Xunit

[<Property>]
let ``Addition is commutative`` (a: int, b: int) =
    MathOperations.add a b = MathOperations.add b a

[<Property>]
let ``Subtraction is not commutative`` (a: int,
```

    b: int) =

    MathOperations.subtract a b <> MathOperations.subtract b a

  ```

By writing unit tests, you can ensure that your code behaves as expected and quickly identify issues as you make changes.

#### Debugging e Profiling

Debugging and profiling are essential practices for identifying and fixing bugs and performance issues in your applications.

1. **Using the Visual Studio Debugger:**

   Visual Studio provides a powerful debugger for .NET applications, including F#.
  ```

- **Setting Breakpoints:**

Set breakpoints in your code by clicking in the margin next to the line numbers. The debugger will pause execution when it reaches a breakpoint.

- **Stepping Through Code:**

Use the "Step Over" (F10), "Step Into" (F11), and "Step Out" (Shift+F11) commands to navigate through your code.

- **Inspecting Variables:**

Hover over variables to see their values or use the "Locals" and "Watch" windows to inspect variables and expressions.

2. **Logging:**

Logging is an essential tool for understanding the flow of your application and diagnosing issues.

```fsharp
open System

let logMessage message =
    printfn "[%s] %s" (DateTime.Now.ToString("o")) message

logMessage "Application started"
```

3. **Using Profiling Tools:**

Profiling helps you understand the performance characteristics of your application and identify bottlenecks.

- **dotnet-trace:**

`dotnet-trace` is a cross-platform tool for collecting performance traces.

```sh
dotnet tool install --global dotnet-trace
dotnet-trace collect --process-id <pid>
```

Analyze the collected trace with PerfView or other performance analysis tools.

- **Visual Studio Profiler:**

Visual Studio includes a profiler that provides detailed performance metrics for your application.

- **CPU Usage:**

    Identify which methods are consuming the most CPU time.

- **Memory Usage:**

    Analyze memory allocation and identify memory leaks.

- **Concurrency:**

    Understand the concurrency behavior of your application and identify contention points.

4. **Using JetBrains dotTrace:**

JetBrains dotTrace is a powerful profiling tool that provides detailed insights into your application's performance.

- **Sampling:**

Profile the application using sampling to get an overview of performance hotspots.

- **Tracing:**

Use tracing to

get detailed call stacks and timings for each method.

- **Timeline:**

Analyze the timeline of your application's execution to understand the flow of events and identify delays.

5. **Using BenchmarkDotNet for Performance Testing:**

BenchmarkDotNet is a library for benchmarking .NET code. It helps you measure and compare the performance of different methods.

Adding BenchmarkDotNet:

```sh
dotnet add package BenchmarkDotNet
```

Writing Benchmarks:

```fsharp
```

```fsharp
open BenchmarkDotNet.Attributes
open BenchmarkDotNet.Running

type Benchmarks() =

    [<Benchmark>]
    member _.Add() =
        MathOperations.add 1 2

    [<Benchmark>]
    member _.Subtract() =
        MathOperations.subtract 2 1

[<EntryPoint>]
let main argv =
    BenchmarkRunner.Run<Benchmarks>() |> ignore
    0
```

```

**Running Benchmarks:**

```sh
dotnet run -c Release
```

This command runs your benchmarks and provides a detailed report of the results.

Designing applications in F# involves a combination of organizing your code, writing
```

unit tests, and performing debugging and profiling. By following best practices for code organization, you can create modular, maintainable, and scalable applications. Implementing unit tests ensures the correctness and reliability of your code, while debugging and profiling help you identify and fix issues efficiently.

This guide has provided a comprehensive overview of these practices with practical examples. By mastering these techniques, you can develop robust F# applications that meet the demands of modern software development.

Index

1. Introduction to F# pg.4

2. Guide to Installing F pg.22

3. Basic Syntax of F#: Variables and Data Types pg.32

4. Fuctions pg.53

5. Pattern matching and list comprehension pg.58

6. Record and tuple pg.62

7. If-then-else e match pg.67

8.Recursion pg.71

9.higher-order functions pg.76

10.Asynchronous and Parallel Programming in F# pg.80

11. Using Libraries and Frameworks in F# pg.101

12.Designing Applications in F# pg.119

www.ingramcontent.com/pod-product-compliance
Lightning Source LLC
Chambersburg PA
CBHW071926210526
45479CB00002B/576